Oh, How Waffle!
Riddles You Can Eat

Judith Mathews *and* **Fay Robinson**
pictures by
Carl Whiting

Albert Whitman & Company
Morton Grove, Illinois

To whom did the riddle writers
dedicate their book?
Each other!

And thanks, Maria and Anna! J.M. F.R.

To my wife and best friend, Margaret. C.W.

Library of Congress Cataloging-in-Publication Data

Mathews, Judith.
    Oh, how waffle! : riddles you can eat/Judith Mathews
and Fay Robinson; illustrated by Carl Whiting.
    p. cm.
    Summary: A collection of riddles and jokes about food
and eating, including "What fruit do gorillas sleep on at
camp? Ape-ricots."
    ISBN 0-8075-5907-5
    1. Riddles, Juvenile. [1. Riddles. 2. Jokes. 3. Eating
customs—Wit and humor. 4. Food—Wit and humor.]
I. Robinson, Fay. II. Whiting, Carl, ill. III. Title.
PN6371.5.M384 1993
818'.5402—dc20   92 -13478
                                                      CIP
                                                       AC

Text © 1993 by Judith Mathews and Fay Robinson.
Illustrations © 1993 by Carl Whiting.
Published in 1993 by Albert Whitman & Company,
6340 Oakton St., Morton Grove, IL 60053-2723.
Published simultaneously in Canada
by General Publishing, Limited, Toronto.
All rights reserved. Printed in the U.S.A.
10 9 8 7 6 5 4 3 2 1

KNOCK, KNOCK.
Who's there?
Lettuce.
Lettuce who?
Lettuce eat, and we'll tell you some riddles!

Lettuce Eat

What did the dog trainer buy at the deli?
A puppy seed beagle.

What color is a belch?
Burp-le.

What two things can't you have for breakfast?
Lunch and dinner.

What is the heaviest soup in the world?
Won ton.

What always sleeps through dinner?
The nap-kins.

What fruit do gorillas sleep on at camp?
Ape-ricots.

Why did the pig eat with its tail?
All animals eat with their tails. They can't take them off.

What are the best slippers in the world made of?
Banana peels.

PFFTWT!

What instrument only plays sour notes?
The pickle-o.

What do you get when you cross a snowstorm with
a cornfield?
Cornflakes.

What do you get when you cross peanut butter with
an elephant?
An elephant that sticks to the roof of your mouth or
peanut butter that never forgets.

How do you make poison ivy into a vegetable?
Put it in your drier — it will come out spin-itch.

What did the cook say when no one arrived for
breakfast?
"Oh, how waffle!"

What famous speech did the noodle president give?
The Spaghettis-burg Address.

Customer: Waiter! I'm in a hurry! Will my pancakes be
long?
Waiter: No, Sir. They'll be round.

Short and Sweet

What kind of cookies do computers like?
Chocolate micro-chip.

What snack do hot-air balloonists eat?
Raisin' cookies.

Why did the little cookie cry?
Because its parents were a-wafer so long.

What is the most important thing to put into brownies?
Your teeth.

How do you make a cherry turnover?
Tickle its stomach.

How do you keep a cookie's jacket closed?
With ginger snaps.

How did the chef get into the kitchen?
With his cook-key.

Why did the baker make a million doughnuts?
Because she loved the hole business.

Monster Mash

How do you know a vampire has been in the bakery?
The jelly's been sucked out of the jelly doughnuts.

What fruit do vampires like best?
Neck-tarines.

What's the Abominable Snowman's favorite food?
Chili.

What salad do Abominable Snowmen like to eat?
Coldslaw.

What happened to the vegetables in the monster's garden?
They all grue-some.

How did the Halloween witch fix her flat bicycle tire?
With a pump-kin.

What do Halloween monsters eat for lunch?
Grilled cheese-and-witches.

How did the giant disguise himself?
He jumped into a can of shortening.

What did the monster eat after its teeth were cleaned?
The dentist.

When is a turkey most like a ghost?
When it's a-goblin'.

What do ghosts choose at the candy counter?
Boo-ble gum.

What do scaredy-cats eat for breakfast?
Bagels with scream cheese.

Foodles

Guess what these foodles are:

A hot potato

Three broccoli spears playing red rover

The lima beans you didn't eat last year

The last portrait of Humpty Dumpty

View from above: a man in a sombrero frying an egg

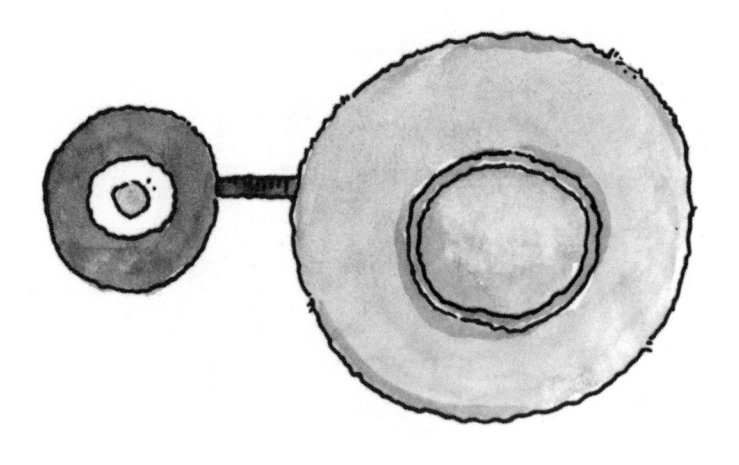

Three pieces of spaghetti run over by a steamroller

View from above: a glass of soda pop

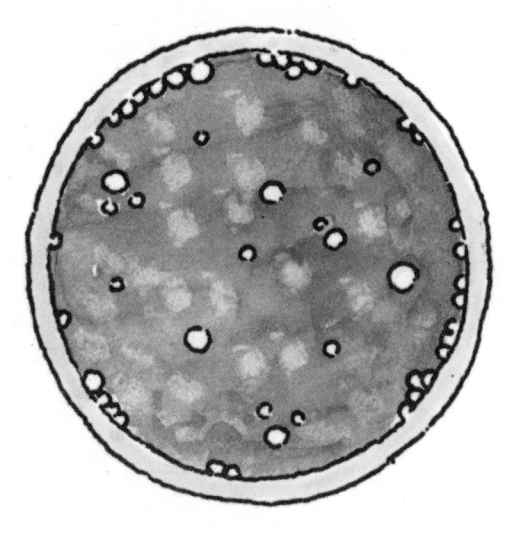

Strawberry shake

The world bubble-gum blowing champion

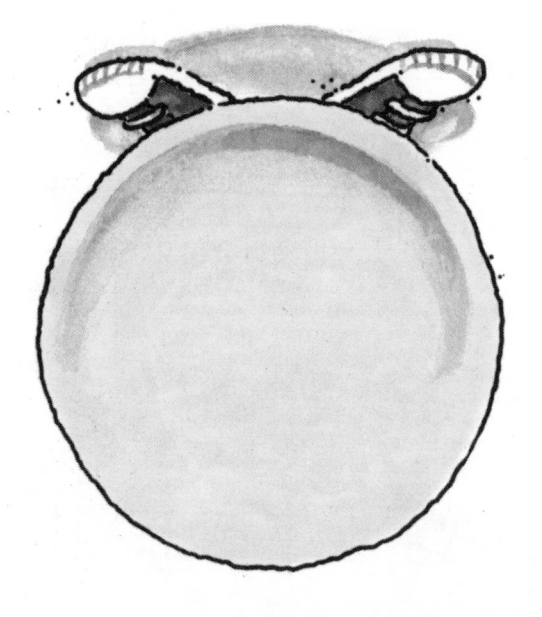

View from the inside of a shark's mouth

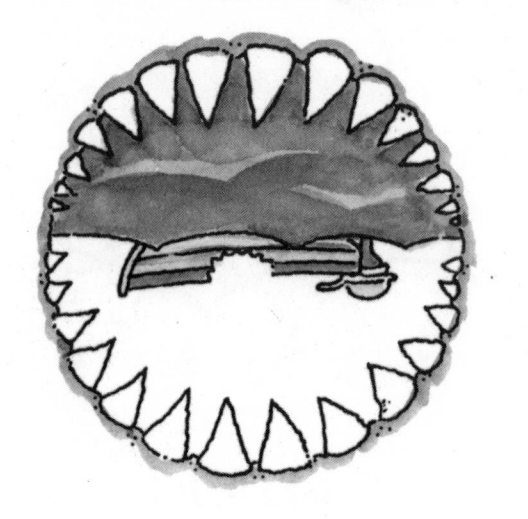

Garden of Eatin'

Why is Santa Claus such a great gardener?
Because he likes to hoe-hoe-hoe.

What is the best way to raise carrots?
Take hold of the tops and pull.

When is a peach a vegetable?
When you have dropped it. (Squash!)

Why did the man find an earring in his salad?
It came off while the salad was dressing.

What did the surgeon remove from her salad?
The kidney beans.

What vegetable is most like a dog?
Collie-flower.

How do you catch a runaway horse?
Hide behind a tree and make a noise like an oat.

What goes up in the air green and comes down red?
A watermelon.

Say "Cheese!"

What do cheeses say when they have their pictures taken?
"People!"

What is the most important use for cowhide?
To hold the cow together.

Which has more legs, one cow or no cow?
No cow. One cow has four legs, but no cow has more than that!

Why was the baby raised on monkey milk?
It was a baby monkey.

What happened when Mrs. Moofle found a goat in the refrigerator?
It turned to butt-er.

How can you tell that a camel has been in the refrigerator?
By the hoofprints in the cream cheese.

How can you keep from getting that sharp pain in your eye when you drink cocoa?
Take the spoon out of the cup.

What did the calf say after breakfast?
"Udder-ly delicious!"

What kind of cars do rich chicken farmers drive?
Egg Rolls.

Who grants wishes to unhappy cheeses?
The dairy godmother.

Clementine: What's the difference between a
container of yogurt and a container of motor oil?
Clarence: I don't know.
Clementine: Boy, I'd hate to send you to the store for
yogurt!

Grub-a-Dub-Dub

Why won't sharks eat clowns?
Because they taste funny.

Customer: Do you serve crabs here?
Waiter: Sure we do — crabs, grouches, anybody!

Why didn't the hermit crab share his candy?
Because he was shell-fish.

How do jellyfish make their jelly?
With ocean currents.

SQUISH

Why is sole the best fish to eat?
Because if you can't finish it, you can put it on your feet.

Why wasn't the octopus invited for dinner?
Because he always eight everything.

How can you cook while surfing?
Use a micro-wave.

How do you make a rock band salad?
With tune-a fish and mayo-noise.

What's the easiest thing to catch when you go ice-fishing?
A cold.

What did the octopus have for lunch?
A peanut butter and jellyfish sandwich.

What fish do balding men prefer?
Hairing.

What game do little fishes play?
Salmon Says.

Dish and Dat

What football event takes place in the kitchen?
The Salad Bowl.

Who keeps track of the cookies you eat?
The kitchen counter.

What happened when the general threw a grenade into the kitchen?
Linoleum Blown-apart.

What would happen if you swallowed your soup spoon?
You wouldn't be able to stir.

Why shouldn't you tell jokes in the kitchen?
Because the dishes might crack up.

Silverware drawer: Doctor, doctor! Why does my
throat hurt?
Doctor: It's u-tonsils.

Who advises the kitchen president?
The Cabinet.

What did the pitcher say when the ice cubes fell on
the floor?
"You need glasses!"

Snicker Snacks

Why couldn't the chef reach the stove?
He was a short order cook.

How do you keep pigs away from your party?
Make it a barbecue.

How do you keep spaghetti from sliding off your plate?
Use tomato paste.

What vegetables do hokey-pokey dancers like best?
Turn-hips.

Why did the farmer stomp on her garden?
She wanted to grow mashed potatoes.

Where does Superman shop for food?
At the supermarket, of course!

What happens when baby sheep eat light bulbs?
They turn into lamps.

Clementine: The doctor just told me I have a food allergy.
Clarence: What are you allergic to?
Clementine: Cashews.
Clarence: Gesundheit!

The Last Bite

A farmer was on his way to market with his prize duck and a sack of corn when he found a wild wolf. He decided to capture the wolf to take to the zoo. He needed to cross a river, but his small boat could hold only himself and one item. How did he cross without leaving the wolf alone to eat the duck or the duck alone to eat the corn?

On trip one, he took the duck across and left it there. On trip two, he took the wolf across, *but brought the duck back to where he started.* **On trip three, he left the duck and took the corn across. On trip four, he took the duck across!**

Lulu ate something for dinner. First, she threw away
the outside and cooked the inside. Then she ate the
outside and threw away the inside. What was it?

Corn on the cob.

A hungry monkey was tied to a rope ten feet long.
Thirty feet away, there was a big bunch of bananas.
How did the monkey get to them?

He walked right over to the bananas. *(Who said the
other end of the rope was tied to anything?)*

A man was locked in a room for six months with nothing but a mattress and a calendar. How did he manage to survive?

He drank water from the springs in the mattress and ate the dates off the calendar.

Every morning, a farmer had eggs for breakfast, but she didn't own any chickens, and she never got eggs from anybody else's chickens. Where did she get the eggs?

From her ducks.